Underground

(Notes toward an Autobiography)

OTHER POETRY BOOKS BY PATRICK LAWLER:

A Drowning Man Is Never Tall Enough, University of Georgia Press, 1990.

Reading a Burning Book, Basfal Books, 1994.

Feeding the Fear of the Earth, Many Mountains Moving Press, 2006.

Trade World Center, Ravenna Press, 2012.

FICTION BY PATRICK LAWLER:

Rescuers of Skydivers Search Among the Clouds, Fiction Collective Two, forthcoming 2012.

The Meaning of If (Short Stories) Four Way Books, forthcoming 2014.

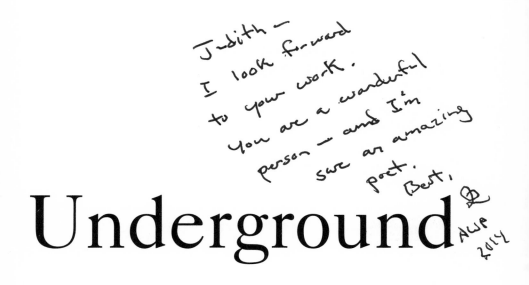

Judith —
I look forward
to your work.
You are a wonderful
person — and I'm
sure an amazing
poet. Best,
PL
AWP
2012

Underground

(Notes toward an Autobiography)

Poems by
Patrick Lawler
with an interview

Patrick Lawler

Many Mountains Moving Press
Philadelphia, Pennsylvania
2012

© All rights reserved. Published 2012.
Manufactured in the United States of America.

Published by Many Mountains Moving Press.
http://mmminc.org.

Editors' Special Project Series, Number 1.

Many Mountains Moving Press titles are distributed by Small
Press Distribution, http://www.spdbooks.org.

Publishers Cataloging-in-Publication Data:
—2nd printing.
ISBN-13: 978-1-886976-27-6

Cover design by John Novak.

Text design and backcover design by Jeffrey Ethan Lee.

Copyediting by Brian Brodeur.

Acknowledgments

Grateful acknowledgment is made to the following journals
and other publications, in which some of these poems and the
interview appeared, occasionally in different forms:

The Interview with Patrick Lawler appeared in *The Bitter Oleander
Volume 15, No. 1.*

"Whole Poems" and "Mickey Mantle Sees Isabelle Allende
Holding The Head Of Hermann Hesse As He Dreams Of
Mother Eve" were collected in *Feeding the Fear of the Earth*, Many
Mountains Moving Press, 2006.

"The Front," "Prison Guard," and "A Drowning Man Is Never
Tall Enough" were collected in *A Drowning Man Is Never Tall
Enough,* University of Georgia Press, 1990.

"How to b a Man (Assembly)" and "Carmen Basilio" appeared
in *Scythe Journal,* Vol. 2.

"(sleep)" appeared in *(reading a burning book),* BASFAL Books,
1994.

"Nigger" first appeared in *Many Mountains Moving: a literary journal
of diverse contemporary voices, Vol. VII, No. 1* (2006).

"Living on Burrowed Time" appeared in *Blackbird: an online
journal of literature and the arts, Vol. 7, No. 2,* Fall 2008, archived at
http://www.blackbird.vcu.edu/v7n2/poetry/lawler_p/burrowed.htm

"At One of my Father's Funerals, I was Humphrey Bogart"
appeared in *Salt Hill Journal, No. 25.*

DEDICATION

FOR MY FATHER,
My Mother, Mike, Mary Ellen, Anne, Colleen

And a special thank you to Jeffrey Ethan Lee, Tim Hayes & Paul Roth.
Paul, you brought my words out of the cellar.
Tim, you brought my soul out of the cellar.
Jeff, you brought the book out of the cellar.

With (L)ots (o)f Gratitude
Ned, Judy, Jack

And Not to Be O(ver)looked
Colleen

CONTENTS

II.

III. Epilogue

Editor's Preface

by Jeffrey Ethan Lee

When I first read Patrick Lawler's 2009 interview with Paul B. Roth in *The Bitter Oleander Volume 15, No. 1,* it was like a prose poem at an adagio tempo, but it was also like a memoir. It was pointed, profound, wry and artful moreso than any other interview I had ever read. It grew more fascinating because it was like discovering the author's notes toward an autobiography, and these notes showed that many of his greatest poems, especially those about his father, were more literally autobiographical than I would have ever imagined. And with these illuminating notes, his poems became far more compelling.

Soon I felt it would do a great service for the poems and the interview to gather them into a book. In the light of the interview, the poems became like a memoir made of poems. Meanwhile, the interview was so poetic that it was like prose poetry made by following the rules of memoir. So this book has evolved as a kind of a poetic autobiography about growing up underground, literally, with a father whose repressed traumas shaped a whole family. That underground life reminds one of what Auden once said of Yeats, "Mad Ireland hurt you into poetry." One is also reminded of Sharon Olds' insightful, wise, and sympathetic portrayals of her father, which inspired Patrick Lawler's work for decades. This book shows one way that a son honestly and ultimately accepts a father, even with all of his torments, and becomes a man. It is a remarkable dual portrait of a son and a father that also shows the longterm consequences of wars, especially the unexpected sufferings caused by wars.

In the end, one increasingly admires the author who finds the courage to transform his compassion for a father into ever greater levels of insight. Including many notes of irony, humor, and even hope, the poems and the prose resonate with astonishing visions and, ultimately, wisdom.

But before this book could go anywhere, I had to share this idea with the author, whom I had gotten to know after editing and publishing *Feeding the Fear of the Earth* in 2006. He ultimately agreed that this was a worthwhile project after I put together a few of the poems in this book with some excerpts of the interview. So many thanks are due to Patrick Lawler and Paul B. Roth, and many others who have granted their permissions. Without all of their help, this book would never have been possible.

I

I

The Lawler family.

"I admit that twice two makes four is an excellent thing, but if we are to give everything its due, twice two makes five is sometimes a very charming thing too."
                                                    —Fyodor Dostoevsky

From the 2009 *Bitter Oleander* Interview

§§§§§§§§§§§§§§§§§§§§§§§§§§§§§§§§§

PBR: *Maybe you could start us off by addressing those earlier influences that have led you to the kind of poetry and fiction you're writing today.*

PL: I could pretend that I had many rich literary influences at a young age—ones that permanently inspired me, goaded me, stained me. But there were other influences that I can never shake, that I will always wear, and that will always wear me—like a dusty coat.

As a child I lived in a cellar for seven years. We had intended to live in a house like everyone else, but my father broke his back and only the cellar was finished. So for seven years we lived inside an unfinished life with a tarpaper roof and small rectangles for windows. We lived inside the shadow of a house. When I talk to people about the cellar, no one understands. The cellar is not a metaphor. The cellar is dirt turned into a beautiful scar.

You see the world differently when you look out a cellar window. I cannot help it—in everything I write there is a cellar.

I rarely believe in the above, but I adamantly cling to my belief in the beneath.

In those days, I wanted to be something, but my destiny was to be a root. Because my father told me not to eat, so my siblings would have more to eat, I substituted writing for food. Writing was my house.

There was an animal that lived with us, and it was scary and it was hope.

Whole Poems

In Cambodia they have a thriving industry
in wheelchairs and artificial limbs.
Thousands of landmines are hidden
in pockets of earth
throughout the country—Claymores
and Chinese models.

In the '50s my father broke his back,
fell off a ladder while he was welding
at a chemical plant. For years
he had to wear a back brace and fight
a Workman's Compensation case
he barely won.

If you walk in Cambodia, you are in danger:
The antipersonnel detonating devices.
The trip mechanisms. The booby traps.
The Soldier's Manual of Common Tasks says:
Install the Claymore facing the center
of mass of a kill zone. The fragments spray
and rip and cut. With patient malice,
the mines wait for years,
thinking all the time their meaning
is undermined until finally
they exuberantly burst. The Chinese model
is propelled upward out of the ground
and reaches a level about the height
of a child's face.

With his broken back, my father didn't work
for years while my mother saved
Green Stamps and we lived in a cellar.

Instead of a house, we lived in a stump.
A cave with a flat tarpaper roof.
With tiny rectangular windows too far
above our heads, too small to let in any light.
Green Stamps like moss
grew all over the tables.

The ex-soldiers and farmers and mothers
and school children drag the lower parts
of their bodies like sacks
along the roads to Phnom Penh.

My father's back brace looked like the rib cage
of a prehistoric reptile—like something
you'd find in a Spanish monastery
during the Inquisition.
I didn't want to look at it.

There are two messages here:
whatever stays in the earth is dangerous
and whatever stays in the earth will save us.

And, of course, there's something else.
In a lab in Massachusetts researchers
are growing human ears on the backs of mice.

Scientists grow the tissue by first creating
an ear-like scaffolding of porous,
biodegradable polyester fabric. Human
cartilage cells are placed throughout the form,
which is then implanted on the back of a
hairless mouse. I wonder

what would grow out of my father's back.

I've always been aware I had a certain destiny.
Right now, I'm supposed to be in Cambodia,
making artificial limbs. I'd make elaborate
prosthetic devices. I'd gather gears and grease
and grinding things, levers and wheels.
I'd work with tubing, haywire, parts of a red
bonnet. I'd make limbs from small engines
and balsam and wax. I'd make windmills.
I'd work with putty and glue, with tintype
and spokes, guitar strings, and plastic.

I'd gather kindling and gourds—
the insides of clocks, tassels, colored ribbon.
I'd whittle crutches into ships.
I'd gather things that sparked
when they rubbed together. I'd take out
the thin insides of pens for veins.

What I want is delicate machinery to carry
pain. What I want are carousels
for fingers, music boxes for hands.

I say: Rise. Get up. Please, walk now.

But my father digs his way down into
his house, and my mother dreams of birds,
collecting them in books. And me?

Whole legs grow out the backs of mice.
Whole poems rip out the back of my father.

From the 2009 *Bitter Oleander* Interview
§ §

PL: Because we didn't have any books, we didn't have any words, and because we didn't have any words, I started writing my own dictionary. Everything that I have ever written has come from a box of words I wrote when I was young—even what I am writing now was waiting for me in that box.

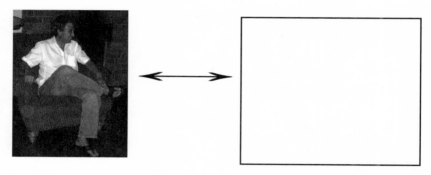

My father was an alcoholic. I never thought I was capable of being a poet. Sure I could write poetry, but to be a poet required more courage, more vision, more words. I could dazzle and entertain, and I was brilliantly adept in my abilities to distract—a little sleight of hand while the real dangerous things were happening behind the mirror.

The cellar was actually the foundation of my grandparents' house that had once burned down. So there was history in the big rocks that made up the cellar, a kind of family hunger, and there was this strange odor of burning that clung to the roof that had once been a floor.

When I think of immersion or resurrection or redemption, it is not an abstraction. These are things that dwell in the cellar— that come out of the cellar when they are not expected.

How to b a Man (Assembly)

Fearful I will be led in
directions I never intended,

I think of my father
being lost in New Guinea.
It was during World War II.
He was on a mission—a patrol.
For a week he wandered in the jungle.

Only two of them came back.

My father said he could
not remember any of it.
Amnesia, he said.

Sometimes, when my father wasn't drunk,
he'd wake up shaking and screaming.
And we knew New Guinea
was trying to get out.

Joseph Campbell tells of a New Guinea
ritual where six or so boys
in their initiation into manhood
make love to this woman dressed as a deity
under a roof of enormous logs.

I often wondered what happened
to my father for those seven days.
Suppose everything I ever was
came out of what was hidden
in my father's head.

He would show us pictures of aborigines.
He also had this one picture
of a man who'd just had his head
cut off. It lay in his lap
with two spurts of blood
shooting from his neck.
A decapitated Buddha.
He could never tell us much
about the picture. Who was the victim?
Who was the man who swung the axe?

We looked at the picture
the same way we looked at our father:
with disgust and awe—
with a kind of reverence.

According to Campbell, while the last
boy was making love to the woman,
the heavy log roof would collapse
killing the couple—a union of beginning
and end, of begetting and death.

My father always wanted me
to write a novel about his life.
But the only thing I ever cared about
was what had happened in New Guinea.
How many people died? How did they die?
What did my father do? What did he see?

My father's whole life collapsed
in those buried memories.

Later, according to Campbell,
the couple who had made love
and died are pulled out from

under the heavy logs and eaten.
That's what we do with the great
mysteries that surround us.
We devour them or they devour us;
we make them part
of us or we're lost inside them forever.

If I were to write that novel,
it would be about death and sex and time.
It would occur in the middle
of a rainforest—in a sacred spot
where death could occur at any moment.

And it would begin and end with these words:
"All my life I will be afraid I'm lost.
All my life I will be afraid I'm found."

And I am there
in my father's life, sitting crosslegged
with my head lying in my lap.
Maybe I am a man
who has just made love to a deity.
Maybe I am a man
whose head has fallen off.

The whole mystical green world
spins around me. Confused with fever,
my father arrives, dazed, jittery.
I want to offer him something to eat
and tell him it is ok to be afraid. I want
to warn him not to leave this place.

The author's father, top.

Michael and Patrick Lawler in their cellar.

The Front

I lost my father's war, its cities,
Its general plan, its movement on the map.
The losses are marked with blue pins:
London misplaced at midnight; Stalingrad,
Dresden gone; Hiroshima, a hole dropped
Inside another hole. I can't identify
A single victim
Wrapped inside his own hands.
I lost the part where barbed wire
Was knitted into nations; I lost
The language. The word Treblinka:
The breaking of thin glass.

From the 2009 *Bitter Oleander* Interview

§ §

PBR: *How would you describe your process of writing? Because of your time constraints, do you work spontaneously wherever you are or do you have to be seated at your desk with things around you in a certain order?*

PL: My writing process (please read as "wanting process") always involves arriving at a space that is between places, entering an ecotone—a space between ecosystems, a boundary area with more diversity, more variety, more richness. *Eco* means place and *tone* means tension—two essential aspects of every creative act (a sense of home and a sense of conflict). I attempt to write in the between—between genres, between places, between times. I wish to create in the seam between the elements—between seem and reality, between forgetfulness and memory, between dream and dream. (An ecotone is a hyphen linking wound and scar.)

    I write with one foot in the box and one foot outside the box. I write with one foot in the cellar and one foot in the sky. A poem itself is an ecotone—a place located between shattered story and irradiated image. Both incantation and incarnation. Both centrifugal and centripetal. A vibrating piece of desire that lives some of its moments in the mouth.

    I try to write in the both. To write with both ecstasy and ache so that, if I am successful, contradictory destinations are possible, and I can achieve both obscenity and prayer, both laughter and gravity. (Ecotones are always about fusion and love—and ultimately sex.)

A Drowning Man Is Never Tall Enough

Death was defiance. Death was an attempt to communicate;
people feeling the impossibility of reaching the centre which,
mystically, evaded them; closeness drew apart; rapture faded,
one was alone. There was an embrace in death.
                    —Virginia Woolf

I.
I hear the squish, squish of shoes
As if someone were walking along
The bottom. The drowning man wears
No footprint. Strangeness always.
The tubes of fish thrown upon the shore,
I ignore the craft warnings,
The chiseled water, the dark slice
Of sails. All my line down, I tire
Of ingenuity. The dead
Fish, the stories of the sea written
With the broken pencils of their bones.
I once watched a retarded boy
Turn a button like a moon
Into a button hole. When he
Would go down to the lake, he would
Stuff his pockets and wear heavy shoes.
He would watch the fish, its big
Unintelligent eyes staring
As it thumped its life out against
The side of the boat. The eyes, hard
And small, the heads of black screws.
If we are going to be saved
Let us get it over with quickly.
I pull up anchor, like an aching tooth.

II.

My father carries with him a terrible
Knowledge: words inevitably select
The wrong person to express their meaning.
Now my father writes these crazy stories
Where nothing happens. He says they are
About his life and wants me to read them.
Our lines snarled, we fish on a river.
Along the banks the birds straighten the cricks
In their unusual necks. Beneath us
Fish slip, their bodies like the handles
Of tarnished pots. A storm cloud churns; the water
Kinks. We are inside one of my father's
Stories entitled "Fear of Water."
I am reminded of Nietzsche in his
Impenetrable Turin, writing
His impenetrable prose after
He watched the horse being beaten. "I would
Rather be a Basel professor than God."
Certainly. Even God would agree.
All day things drift by us: photographs
Of weddings; a gold watch, its chain
Trailing behind it; a hat. But there is
Something down there that won't come up. The snag.
I cut myself away.
                              Later we hear
Someone has drowned. I keep looking for my
Father; he, wiser, keeps looking for me.

III.

Leaner than wheat, one day I arrive
Announcing my hobby: denial.
A woman plays the piano,
A gold and rickety music.
I leave the rivers running all night,

Enchanted by the waste, the isolated
Blue of waste. Leaving lives in our
Evaporating fictions; motion holds
Everything in place. One day I arrive,
Announcing my hobby. I am down
By the sea with the singer by the sea.
The sea teeters and turns, circles its own
Secret, the blossom of the self,
The dark onyx of the self.
It sings in the spin and the gimmickry
Of what is created. The drowning
Man stands with dark sobs of oil
On his trousers, on the rag that he
Clutches. He says, "I do not use
The word love enough or use it once
Too often." As always, I leave
Something out: a reason, a plan,
An indispensable middle.
The retarded boy scoops up his
Reflection in the water
And presses it to his face.
My father stands in one of his
Own stories reaching for a word
He knows he'll have to erase: my name.
The voice of the singer by the sea
Turns into sky all around us.
It is summer; the beaches are
Glue golden. There is wakefulness
Even in the stones. The drowning
Man dreams of fish with small, black eyes.
The world stays the same, influenced
By the usual alchemy.
The curious birds, who tilt
And circle, seem never to touch the sky.

From the 2009 *Bitter Oleander* Interview
§§§§§§§§§§§§§§§§§§§§§§§§§§§§§

More than anything, my wanting process [please read as "writing process"] is achieved by creating an artifice—an elaborate and false structure through which and in which I can dream and desire and create.... Intimate archi(text)ures built out of plump body parts and interwoven echolalia with neologisms and pomegranate-like chambers. Rhizomatic and ephemeral. Metabolic and paradoxical. Self-organizing systems. Dissipative structures creating new patterns of coherence and relationship. Once I imagine this complex house, I dig in the cellar. I chip away at the blocks. Free to do anything, I shatter, I burrow, I thrive.

Borderless, I attempt to both relish and undermine the order—the amazingly beautiful lie, and, eventually, if all is successful, I do my stumble-dance on the edge of crashing. (Thus, in composing the answers to this interview, the box has evolved into an external structuring device. It has allowed me to enter territory I would never have been able to imagine. But simultaneously there is a chewing through the seductiveness of the structure, and there is an internal process of deciphering and denial, undermining and disassembling.) Given these experiences, I try never to sit at a desk. Quite frequently I write with the following in mind: To prepare for levitation, place one foot firmly in the air.

CARMEN BASILIO
Welterweight & Middleweight Champion of the World
1955-'56-'57-'58

Carmen Basilio

In the fifth round of his championship fight
with Lennox Lewis, Oliver McCall has a nervous breakdown.
He stands in the middle of the ring, arms at his sides, crying.
The crowd is stunned and booing. The announcers are appalled.

When we were kids, my brother and I
watched the Saturday Night Fights with my father.
He was usually drunk, and my brother and I
would fall asleep by the sixth round. It didn't matter.
It didn't matter that no one was really there to experience any of it.
This was an initiation, and the only thing required was
to have the unconsciousness bathed in black and white.

Once my father took me to see Carmen Basilio
at the War Memorial. My father said, "See.
He just doesn't go down." My father liked that.
Determination. Persistence. Tenacity. Balls.

All these men trying to punch holes in each other's heads.
I saw boxing as majestic and noble, brutal and savage and pure.
Sleazy and sacred. Shamans in sequined rags, intimate with danger
maybe even intimate with death. Dempsey's punches traveled at 135mph.
Ali danced out of Liston's reach as he turned into one animal, and then
        another.
Sugar Ray flickered around the ring. I saw boxing as power and grace,
an elemental beauty sponsored by Gillette.
I saw the ethnic roots, the corporeal music. Blood and cigar smoke.

The fighters stood toe to toe. With chipped lips.
Banging the buckets of their heads. Fattened
and ripped. Scuffed. Unstoppable. The jabs and hooks.
The bobbed and woven. The dance shuffles.

The fists like sledges breaking the body into dust.
Surgery conducted with hammers and chisels.

Once at our town's Fall Festival they had the kids box,
and I was in the ring against this bigger guy who said
he was going to kick my ass.
But he had no way of knowing that I would never
give up. I came out of my childhood with only a few lessons.
And to tell you the truth, I didn't give a shit about winning.
Anybody could win, I decided. If you had the right family.
If you had the right edge. If you were big enough.
Or rich enough. All I cared about was not giving up
no matter what. He could have hit me a million times,
and I'd still be standing in front of him.

And there stood Carmen Basilio as if he'd been pounded with rocks.
His brain beaten into beef. Scar tissue on places no one could see;
damage on places where no one would want to.

Years later Carmen Basilio taught Gym where I went
to college. After sit ups and squat thrusts, he'd hand out the towels.
I don't think anyone there remembered him the way I did,
like somebody who was supposed to be somebody.
Like somebody who wouldn't go down for the count.
His brain a little stripped; his mouth unable to get around all of his words.

When I was young I memorized the names of gangsters
for the same reason I learned the names of fighters.
There was an indescribable beauty in the litany of names:
Muhammed and Rocky. Tiger Flowers and Kid McCoy.
Gentleman Jim and the Brown Bomber. Frazier and Foreman and Griffith.
I knew one day I would need them. I would need to call them from the
        canvas.
I would need to say, "Goddamn it. Help me. I can't do it by myself any
        longer."

24

I didn't know how to weigh the heart. I didn't
have a scale that would tell me about courage or vision or skill.
I didn't know about words. I didn't know how not to be afraid.

As if something is terribly short circuited,
as if everything is drenched in grief and bewilderment,
Oliver McCall stands in the middle of the ring crying.
For radiance? For deliverance? Arm weary, brain weary, heart weary,
he is tired of pummeling whoever it is he pummels:
a man, a mirror, a father who is nowhere to be seen.

I even care less about winning, but now I know
there's a different courage—the kind it takes to say,
even when no one else is around, you can stop hitting me now.

Prison Guard

Every time my father sees me he apologizes

For forgetting to make duplicates of his keys.

All the while he is intent on watching my hands.

It's all right, I explain. When he looks at a butterfly,

My father reaches for his thumbprint. The job did that;

It made him half certain he was only partially there.

Though retired, he still tells the stories:

The tricks played on him at headcount,

The lengthy interrogations over missing spoons,

The flashlight he shot into bed clothes.

My father doesn't leave the trailer anymore.

From the same small window where the night tips in,

He watches. The book with the pictures helps

Him identify the things that he sees: a bird

Landing in a tree like a burglar's shoe,

A lilac, a marigold, an auto.

This way when we're together we have something

To say. But the points we arrive at aren't there.

And after I leave, he wipes what I've touched with a rag.

"Nigger"

The father

brought home the word

nigger

and laid it on the kitchen table
        with his handcuffs and his badge.

A prison guard, he would explain how they would take the civil
rights demonstrators from booking to the cells. In the elevator
they would beat them good. It wasn't clear from his description
whether he threw any punches.

You don't know how hard

I tried

to have another father.

He brought home

a silence slash sermon;

    it filled up the house

                    with two hundred years.

I tried to explain it with sociology, psychology, history. I watched
things die around my father's hands. He once showed me how
to subdue a prisoner. He once showed me how to hit so you
wouldn't leave any bruises. Once a man escaped from my father.
Being taken from a holding cell to a courtroom, the prisoner
got away. The father was never the same. Humiliation collapsed
inside his throat.

            After Malcom X
        and Martin Luther King,
                after a decade of token change,

in a room stuffed with TV-silence.

It was after the divorce, after the children stopped visiting him, after he was diagnosed with throat cancer. He bought a parrot and kept it in a cage. I don't know what words he tried to teach it, but the parrot never said anything. It just sat green and purple in its cage with golden bars as thin as tear ducts. After the father died, his sheriff's patches, like flattened hearts, the ones he wore on the sleeves of his uniform, were shoved in with all his other stuff.

"He once showed me how to hit

so you wouldn't leave

any bruises.

But now I know that's absolutely impossible."

I've seen the documentaries—the courage it took to cross a
bridge against dogs and batons and firehoses. The courage to sit
on a bus or at a lunch counter in Woolworths. The courage to
be a man, to be a woman. To be a man, to be a woman. I want
to say to the person who stumbles out of the elevator: Tell me
my father didn't do this to you. Tell me it was anyone. Tell me it
was me—my two hundred years of cowardice.

This green and purple thing

that slumps inside me.
        Silent and afraid.

"You don't know how hard I tried to have another father."

30

From the 2009 *Bitter Oleander* Interview
§§§§§§§§§§§§§§§§§§§§§§§§§§§§§§§

PL: Most of what I write I do not want anyone to read. I often drag it back into the cellar where the box of words is waiting. (Believe me. This does not want to be read.)

I carry that cellar with me wherever I go. I put a hole in the middle of this answer—that hole is the cellar where I still live. "Don't be afraid of me," the cellar says. I have to say with a poem that I am not a poet. I want to fill up that hole with words—but I have come to realize the space has to exist because that's where the words come from.

PBR: *What kind of similarities or differences exist between this box and the absence out of which everything grows and then ultimately returns?*

PL: A year ago I discovered a large box of words I had gathered when I was much younger. It was crammed full of notes and ideas, poems and short stories I had written from sixteen to twenty-four. Beginnings and middles. Images and words. Scribbles. Whole notebooks. Folders full of yellow paper. Most I had completely forgotten, like letters to a dead self. Accounts of witness and indictments and hope. Dispatches from a dark place. I poked among the patches and detritus. I could not believe what I found. I was cracking open the past—staring into a grave. I couldn't look into it long because some of what was there was still alive.

The box was an alembic where light and dark have sex. A bin haunted by the potential for fire. A place to store gravity. A box with stone walls. A wet well with words beating like the insides of a lake.

I pull out some of the pieces from the box to answer this question:

> From a poem, "For the Lady with the Mouthful of Roses"—
> "Fountains pour forth stones;/Gardens feed the sun."
>
> From a short story, "Come Inside the Rain. We are Inside the
> Rain"—"And he didn't know whether he wanted the rain to
> end—or whether he just wanted to watch the umbrellas go
> up like brains."
>
> A note from a professor: "Please don't show me any more of
> this sort of writing."
>
> A note from another professor: "Unfortunately, I do not con
> sider what you write to be poetry."
>
> One story ends with a rectangular box cut out of it. It was
> supposed to represent the space left from a clipped coupon
> the narrator had sent to the Save Your Life Society.

Now I know that cut out space represented the box that the hole
would eventually reside in. In some ways the hole was waiting for this
question—waiting to swallow it up.

Here is what I have learned: The box eats itself from the inside. It is
waiting for what I will become in order to appreciate where I have
been. The answer is always hungry for the question. If the answer is
a tongue, the question is a mouth.

II

Mickey Mantle Sees Isabelle Allende Holding The Head Of Hermann Hesse As He Dreams Of Mother Eve

•

When I'm in Mexico,
Mickey Mantle
is dying of cancer.
Once I burned
his baseball cards
in a shoebox—
a symbolic gesture
of leaving.

•

The seas are rough around Cancun.
Black flags on all the beaches.

•

Everyday I go looking for a   *milagro*,
miniature figures: body parts, inner
organs, animals. They are offered
to a saint to commemorate
a miracle or to ask the saint's intercession.

•

How do you say:

"I am an American,

and I am prepared

to buy everything you have"?

•

I'm going to go swimming with the dolphins.
I'm going to go diving into the strange—as if words
were a species, as if desire were a species, as if pain
                              were a species.

                              •

                    I dream about
                parachutists
                          in bright colored jump suits
                          falling through the sky.

•

This is the week when we celebrate
dropping the bomb on Hiroshima.
        The usual parades.
Shadow floats. Balloons filled with tears.
Helium carried by men and women
                    with melted hands.

                              •

                    On the way to Tulum,
                    I dive into a cenote,
                    a hole into an underground
                    river, a lavish mouth,
                    a fantastic eye filled
                    with holy water and forgiveness.

        •

        Everyday I look for a   *milagro*,
        little medals made of tin or silver or gold—
        wax or wood or bone.
        If you have a headache,
        the *milagro* will be in the shape of a head.

•

If your heart is hurt,
it will be in the shape of a heart.
You pin them on a saint
and everything is made better.

•

How do you say:
"I am an
American,
and I will sell you
everything
you will never
need"?

•

I am afraid I will not find
the appropriate   *milagro*.

•

It is 8:15 a.m. August 6, 1945.
A six-year-old boy waits
on the platform of the Hiroshima Station.
He waits for a train that vanishes as it arrives.

•

I dream about parachutists—
1,000s of them in brilliant yellows,
whites, and oranges dropping out of the sky
in the field next to the house
I grew up in as a child.
They are on a secret mission.

37

●

A woman rubs my hair and says it will cost
a certain amount of pesos for the room,
a certain amount of pesos for her body.
        She offers me the cenote.
The delicious waters of her skin.

●

A Mexican friend and his wife feed me
in a bungalow of sticks and tar paper.
La casa de mis suenos. They are proud.
She is pregnant.   I am American.

●

I needed someone else other than my father
to be my father. Mickey Mantle
stumbles around the bases.

        The ball will never land.

●

I look for a *milagro* for Mickey Mantle—
something in the shape of lungs or wings.

●

Fifty years ago we set the sky on fire.
        Robert Lewis, the copilot
of the Enola Gay,   writes in his journal,
"My God, what have we done?"

●

I look for
milagros
with melted

hands.

●

It is 1961 and I am dying.
My eyes don't need me any longer.
It is 1995 and the parachutists
come and announce
I've been dead a long time.

●

I want   to give   my Mexican friend
a *milagro*   the size   of a fetus.

●

The sea's shoulders are collapsing
under the pinned moon.
One-hundred-fifty-thousand people
come out of the sea waving black flags.

●

How do you say:
"I am an
American"?

●

In Hiroshima they float
brightly colored umbrellas and lanterns
on Hiroshima's seven rivers
to remember the dead, to remember those
who drowned trying to cool
their burning bodies.

●

Tonight, there will be an aluminum moon
pinned to the sky.
I won't go swimming with the dolphins.
It's 1995,   and America
will put Mickey Mantle in a shoebox.

From the 2009 *Bitter Oleander* Interview

§§§§§§§§§§§§§§§§§§§§§§§§§§§§§§§

PBR: *When you are there in your process of doing and not doing, has the fact that you're getting older made it any easier for you?*

PL: Not sure. I have a couple of thoughts that need to be sorted through:

1. I have a fear of immortality. I'm not kidding. Mortality is reassuring—dependable. There like a stump. But when I go to sleep, I am aware there is always the possibility that when I wake I will discover I am eternal. Then, what? I wonder.

2. My favorite quote by Thoreau appears at the end of the chapter in *Walden*—"Where I Lived and What I Lived for": "The intellect is a cleaver; it discerns and rifts its way into the secret of things. My instinct tells me that my head is an organ for burrowing, as some creatures use their snout and forepaws, and with it I would mine and burrow my way through these hills. I think that the richest vein is somewhere hereabouts; so by the divining-rod and thin rising vapors I judge; and here I will begin to mine." Thus, Descartes' I-think-therefore-I-am duality is shattered. The think-part is a burrower. We need to think with that animal part of the brain. With souls and words and intellect we get down in the dirt and tunnel.

3. Gabriel Garcia Marquez writes in *One Hundred Years of Solitude*: "Thus they went on living in a reality that was slipping away, momentarily captured by words, but which would escape irremediably when they forgot the values of the written letters." Words are DNA—they contain genetic instructions and this storage of information allows for the transcription of our world.

4. At the cellular level we are in a constant state of transformation. We are not the same person we were three months ago. About 1% of our body is new each day. Through breakdowns and break-throughs, we are in a constant state of renewal. When you see me again, of course, you won't recognize me. I will be a river wearing a hat.

5. I have a fear that words are mortal. Approximately 6,000 languages are spoken on earth, and 3,000 of them are threat-ened. Once a word dies the part of the world the word uniquely described also dies. In the staggering number of language extinc-tions, the final word topples over in the mouth of its last speaker.

6. Because I come from a (cell)ar, I always wear my dirt coat. I am in a constant state of evolution. Change comes at us in bursts of brokenness and beauty. Souls crash into little tumors of light. Words prepare my mortality for me. They allow the animal part of me to crawl out of my mouth and stagger back to the begin-ning—each cell returning to the cellar. I wear my burrowing brain in order to enter the secret of things.

(sleep)

> We share a world when we are awake; each sleeper is in
> a world of his own.
> —Herakleitos

(My father,
Schooled in the art of sleeping,
Slept. A narcoleptic, he would doze off
At the drop of anything, at the drop
Of a snowflake, at the drop
Of his slow gray hat.

He slept through the depression
While other men floated out of ten-story windows.
He slept through Normandy Beach.
He slept through my sister's ringlets,
My mother's villanelles, the unfinished

Crossword puzzles of our conversations.
Through Eisenhower and Sputnik,
He crumbled up beneath his hat.

Sleep fell around him. It spilled out
Of his shoes, out of his coat's big pockets.
He left it behind in his footsteps.
One saw it in the brittle eyes
Of chickens when he passed. One heard it
In the stomach of a cat. One thought
Of it when reading Chekhov.

Whenever I saw the color black,
It was my father sleeping.)

What is most *to be feared* is insomnia. The doctor has
not spoken to me about it, nor have I spoken of it to him.
But I am fighting it myself by a very, very strong dose of
camphor in my pillow and mattress.

—Van Gogh

(I can't sleep.
A wounded man is in the garden.
We have peered into the grave
Formed by his hands, the glaze of his late
Eyes. We must notify someone.

Try a bath of Lime Flower, a sachet
Of chamomile. The Countess of Soissons
Even had cushions for her thumbs.

Drink sweet marjoram, hawthorn, and melissa.

No.

There is a strange light,
The sunset draining away
Over Cross Lake.

Sometimes we see everything clearly:
The magpie's nest in a tall acacia,
The sunflower in its false fever, the dull

Orange of the freshly cut earth.
An avenue of pink flowering chestnuts.

Yet we mustn't let clarity deceive.
The wounded man dreams of our demise,
Does the dance of our departure.)

No small art is it to sleep: it is necessary to keep
awake all day for that purpose.
                                —Nietzsche

(All wrong from the start, I began
By separating what is from what is,
Wondering in unearned astonishment.
I live lavishly off what is lost.

My father sleeps in his dark suits;
My mother walks in a pink

Haze. It is late at night,
And I am reading Nietzsche, his quest
For the depth
Of God.

My brother and sisters talk
In their blue sleep, a chorus
Of nonsense and light, their voices
Moving like incest
From bedroom to bedroom.

All day my father reads the burning
Book; all night he writes it.

Nietzsche had his tray of sedatives
Against his insomnia: Chloral hydrate
And Veronal. What keeps the words
Coming? The dialogue
Winds through the thick night air.

The solipsist sleeps.
I keep whispering a word until
It grows smaller and smaller.)

Nothing frightens me more than the false serenity
of a sleeping face.
                    —Cocteau

(There is a story
Here somewhere, but I won't
Let it out.

My mother would rub herself with essence
Of benzoin; she would scent her sheets
With orange blossom, heliotrope and
Oil of bergamot. Still she would
Sleepwalk in her pink flannel gown.

My mother descends the octave
Of stairs, a crucifix hanging
From her neck,
Settling between her breasts—
The round heads of the silver
Nails delicately driven.)

But, speaking of "resemblances," I mean that dream presentations are analogous to the forms reflected in water, as indeed we have already stated. In the latter case, if motion in the water be great, the reflexion has no resemblance to its original, nor do the forms resemble the real objects. Skillful, indeed, would he be in interpreting such reflexions who could rapidly discern, and at a glance comprehend, the scattered and distorted fragments of such forms, so as to perceive that one of them represents a man, or a horse, or anything whatever.
—Aristotle

(Places my father did not sleep:
Greece and Rangoon. Moscow. Madrid.
He did not sleep
In Vancouver or Martinique.

He never snored
In the musical air of Helsinki.

Trapped in his geography, he moved
Along the rich black borders of sleep,
Guided by those first cartographers,
Who found emptiness in all the wrong places,
Who created the world out of chasms
And crossroads. When they stopped

Dreaming, there was the air's edge.
My father did not fall asleep in Africa.
He did not fall asleep in Dublin
Though he wished he had.

It does not seem possible:
I find the world everywhere.
Here is a man. There is a horse.
This is anything whatever.)

(My father understood the sleep of animals.
A crow is the stone of sleep. Coal
Is the bird of sleep. This is life.

This is life.

The crocodiles open up like car
Hoods; the elephants are the color
Of dented garbage cans.
The spigots of the birds' necks
Whistle over the emptiness.
This is life. This is life.
A cross old bass. Trout
Sleeping like the throats of women.
The breath of black bees.

Listen to the parrot wondering
If this is Africa. The green gum
In its veins wonders.
Look, the crocodiles sleep like sneakers.
Something is rocking inside them.
The heart. The heart is almost

Extinct. My mother's sleep turns into snow;
My father's sleep turns into nothing.

Glub. Glub.
The hippopotamus walks like
A diplomat with a secret mission.)

My dreams are not me; they are not Nature, or the
Not-me: they are both. They have a double conscious-
ness, at once sub- and ob-jective.
—Emerson

(It is a regular dream with the usual
Things happening. Europe is sleeping
On trains. Men are wearing sleeve garters.
Women sweep past the closed
Doors of the Pullman cars.

The body of a train conductor:
Ticket stubs clenched in his hands.

Then Freud shows up
Out of one of his dreams.
The barber pole spins its slow blood.
The lotions, the clippers, the canisters
Of combs. He looks haggard—
His coat like a dusty road.

Then I am sitting in a red chair,
The color of bad blood.
The white sheet snaps stormily.
Bottles of liquid like green secrets.
Chunky shaving mugs. The snick
Of scissors around my ears.

There's a sign over the mirror.

Someone, hunched and uncertain, walks
Through the door, but the bell doesn't
Ting. A mistake has been made.
Even when dead, Laius lives.)

(This is the poem my mother walks through,
The poem my father sleeps through.
I think it was Kepler who discovered
The way the moon hooks into the darkness.

My father would have taught
Me that, if he hadn't had his own
Crosspurposes, his own
Black world to step back into.

I squeeze my eyes until all that remains
Of the night is the night's dark juices.
I took this method from my father
As I watched his knotted breath,
The scratched air around his body.
Is is also *was*.

He slept through Cantigny and Belleau
Wood; he slept through gilt-edged securities,
The Teapot Dome, and Al Capone.
He slept through the landing
Of Lindbergh at Le Bourget aerodrome.
He slept through the moon

That hung over Hanoi.)

Our life is two-fold: Sleep hath its own world,/ A
boundary between the things misnamed/ Death and
existence; Sleep hath its own world,/ And a wide realm
of wild reality.
                                        —Byron

(During the moonwalk when my father was sleeping,
My mother applauded. She watched the astronauts
Chug along in their puffy gray suits. They'd almost
Drift off in a lazy leap as if nothing could
Hold them. Then they'd return and suddenly stick.

It was late at night, the voices of my brother
And sisters winding blue through the air. My father
Woke and called me. The air was blue and
False and blue. It was as if he were lying
In a hole. The moon was glued to the windows.

If I had taken one step in any direction, I would have drifted
away.)

> The sleeper turns into himself and falls back into the womb.
> —Roheim

(First the sky is the sky.
It is always in the middle of itself.
Storm clouds or clearing.
Scarred with light. Simply scared.
Some things that happen do.
And some things that happen don't.

For example, what we have scraped
Together, dream scraps for genitals,
Dream scraps for hearts,
An uncle's pocket watch
Like a testicle that has stopped.

The doctor arrives with bad news
On his breath. My mother carries
The color blue inside her womb.
Fear: someone will be listening

And I'll have nothing to say.

It is always 3 A.M.
Time: a tower falling toward us
In the dark.)

He giveth his beloved sleep.
—Psalms 127:2

(The wounded man is in the garden.
At first we ignored him, mistaking
His wounds for geraniums.
My wife says we should call someone.
He is turning blue among the flowers'
Crushed throats, the petals
Like scalded flesh, his hands

Twisted in ivy. My wife cannot sleep
Thinking how beautiful
He is becoming. But the garden
Is turning into weeds because she
Can't bear to enter it.
Dandelions and clover. Thistle.
Black Medic. Chickweed. Oxalis.
Yellow Rocket, Veronica, Violets.

I need to enter the names
Of things. I want the word
For the weed that grows
Out of my heart.)

A sense of real things comes doubly strong.
—Keats

(Cross Lake is flickering with sunset.
I am watching the hat of a man
Who is burning. My father sleeps
In a different language. Now he sleeps
In Latin; sometimes he sleeps

In German—the dark cloud of his snoring.

I need to make the visible invisible
Again, so I can see it. Behind me
There are centuries of sleeping.
I am sleeping through Galileo's stars.

I am sleeping through
Paracelsus, Hippocrates, and Newton.

The sixth century sleeps in its own smoke.
The twelfth century sleeps like a monk.
It wonders what God is
For.

The full moon: night's ovulation.)

Even sleeping men are doing the world's business
and helping it along.
                    —Herakleitos

(I am watching a bird rising over
Cross Lake, moving in tight circles.
It has relinquished its mind,
It has abandoned its stumbling logic.

My father is sealed in his sleeping,
Holding onto each ember of pain,
Fearing that nothing else is real.

He inhales and he is part world;
He exhales and it is part him.

My mother, pink and cautious, walks
Along the shore. Her sleep cannot
Contain her. She still knows the dance of air.

And my mother burns
The burning book,
And by that light
We love her.

My wife's body is under a blue sheet,
A wave that won't go by.
My daughter rocks in my arms.
To have a language for less,
To have a music for leaving.

I am losing all ambition: the bird
Pronounces the word sky with its body.)

From the 2009 *Bitter Oleander* Interview
§§§§§§§§§§§§§§§§§§§§§§§§§§§§§§§§

PBR: *So, when you're writing or not writing, not writing or writing, then the urge to write is always the same, always different, but an urge nonetheless from the highest magnitude of imagination you can dial up?*

PL: Maybe dig up is more appropriate.

Anyway.

I find the answer to this question in the long lost box of words.

The story of the minotaur provides two metaphors for two different approaches to creativity.

Either you make a labyrinth to hide the monster, or you fashion wings to allow the child to rise up and fly.

Of course, both approaches have significant problems.

     The monster still needs to be fed.

And the wings if used to their ultimate potential inevitably will have to melt.

The first ambitious poem I ever wrote was called "The Minotaur."

To be a maker (meaning, metaphor, amazement) one must become lost in the labyrinth of one's own making. Aspiring toward the sun, one must eventually plummet into something resembling light.
I think in terms of "books"—no matter what the project (poetry

or story, essay or script). And each "book" must be the same "book")—and each "book" must be utterly different. Each must contain its own passageways and arteries, its own monster, and its own sense of possibility and transformation, its own flying-boy and drowning man.

Every question must lead to a different shaped answer with a constant thread.

I have to admit, my first attempt at something large and labyrinthine, complex and tangled, was an utter failure. The minotaur and the maze never became one. The thread and the wings never became one.

At first it is scary and then it is hopeful: this need to write/not write.

Then there is this moment of revelation: I could never leave that first poem behind me. I never could get out of its mess. I've always been inside that poem picking up pieces of feather. Always fashioning wings from spit and twigs.

I look into the container of writing I thought I lost. Another revelation: The maze is actually a beautifully psychotic box—multi-chambered, inflowing and efferent.

Yes, dig up is definitely more appropriate.

Writing
is both the labyrinth
and the way out of the labyrinth.

Living on Burrowed Time

This morning I saw my dead father-in-law
driving a Pinto. The weird thing is that
it wasn't his car. The dead obviously
don't get to drive the current models.

                    I wanted to yell to him
          about the gas tank exploding,
but then I remembered he was dead,
and warning him didn't make a lot of sense.
Maybe all the dead drive Pintos
with bursting gas tanks, and they tipsily spin into turns
on erupting Firestone tires.
That's got to be part of the fun of being dead.

Death has to take us seriously.
Eventually, we become this fear inside us.
We become our skin which is made of death.
We wear it around us, and our deaths protect us—
with their kindnesses—soft and pliable.

I had a dream once where my grandmother never died.
Everyone thought she was dead, but instead
she moved in with a distant aunt. To visit my grandmother
I had to drive through a quaint dream-size village.

In the dream, I was in my aunt's living room
that looked as if it had been covered with a doily.
The aunt told me my grandmother
was convinced she could talk
to God, but she was determined not to.
In my dream, I expressed my admiration.
"Good for you," I said, and my aunt said,

58

"Don't bother. It's not just God she doesn't talk to."

I'm sure you would agree:
death is the small end of the funnel.

Frequently when I wake up, it takes
a moment to figure out who is alive
and who is dead—who I can expect to bump into
and who I will need to get used to not seeing.

The most embarrassing thing
is to ask a person how so-and-so is
and then be told by their child or spouse or parent,
"You know. They died." "I'm sorry," I say.
"But you were at the funeral."

I can't help it.
Sometimes life and death blur together.

Once my dead father left me a message
on my answering machine.
I wasn't convinced it was him
           because he mumbled.
He seemed to be trying to sell me insurance.
For the first time in my life,
I thought I should be listening to him.

For the moment, at least, I do
all the things death cannot do.
I burrow into what I can burrow into.

Once my father opened an egg
and found his death inside it.
That was just before he got involved in selling insurance.

Of course, I know this poem will be used against me.
All my life I tried not to write it
though it has been waiting for me.
Like my own death, it leans in a doorway,
smoking a cigarette, as cool as James Dean
in a dangerous leather jacket, vulnerable and sexy,
speaking in the softest of burrowings.

I should have asked my father
                            about the premiums.
How much time I'd need to borrow.

        It will be weird having you
        read this after I am dead.
I guess we will just have to get used to it—
all these words detached from us.
All these words softly exploding.

LUNG/air/SCULPTURE

within Aboriginal Murri Dreamings
People and Land IS Law—sustaining
Aboriginal and Rain is my Protein
　　　　　　—Lionel Fogarty

Years after the father died, the boy found his ashtray in the shape of Australia—a silver country with a deep burn mark. A kangaroo bolted to the shores of the Coral Sea. The boy never understood the world that flowed up to the metal beaches.

documents of air

string made
catalog　　　　　of milk

whimsical documents of air

world of
dementia and diamonds

1. aphrodisiacs

2. ships

3. deletions

In Dreamtime, the ancestors emerged from their slumber. Their journeying created the features of the land. Their actions and their singing fashioned the world. When their journeys were finished, they went back into the earth or metamorphosed into the sensuous plants and the animals with their flowering senses.

The ashtray was a souvenir from World War II. Lots of countries had burned centers. Other soldiers from different parts of the war must have purchased ashtrays in the shape of Japan or Dresden or Stalingrad.

words
as nerve
endings

                                         IV tubes
                                          & drizzle

                    I watch
                    the world
                    through   documents of spilled air

The Trails are musical scores etched upon the land—one couplet for each pair of Ancestor's footfalls. An auditory map where the Aborigine only has to repeat the song of the Dreaming. Thousands of meandering and intersecting songlines. A continent crisscrossed with story and music.

The father sat at the kitchen table with a pack of Winstons and a beer, Australia overflowing. And the boy was upstairs in his bedroom practicing yoga. The world tenderly entered and exited both lungs. Lacking the tension of dialectics, the experiment with clarity and connection unsuccessful, they stopped breathing in the world.

Wittgenstein

with his string

The Aborigine believe every Ancestor deposited "spirit children" along the journey. Intercourse with a man prepares the woman for conception. When the woman feels the first movement in her womb, she notes what spot on the earth this occurs, and the elders determine on what songline the "spirit child" entered the womb.

a delicate

Mobile

After years of selling Electrolux, after years of being a prison guard, after breaking his back, after being chased by UFOs when he was drunk, after the divorce, after the trailer, the father was diagnosed with bronchial carcinoma, and the family spent its time in waiting rooms, in hospital lounges, at the foot of a tilted bed. The spot where the child enters the mother's womb determines what clan the child will be born into. The green foam slippers like clouds. The child is forever connected to the conception place by the song, becoming a caretaker of the place and the singing.

A DELICATE

MOBILE

OF OXYGEN

The TV turned to fuzz. Puzzles stacked on corner tables. The child is given the stanzas of the Ancestor's song which were sung on the spot of conception. One patient undergoing radiation for cancer of the throat had two blue crosses marked on his neck. The child is a descendent of the Ancestor and the song, responsible for the journey, the song, and the land.

The man working the puzzle had a piece that should have been the sky if only it would fit.

        mathematics

               of angels

The father was growing unexpectedly, at first, a tangerine, according to the doctor, nurtured until the whole tree followed. The high calcium level turned his mind into clearest air; everything falling through it like sunlight, pale and focused. When Aborigines go on a "Walkabout," they follow a ritual journey along a Dreaming Trail, walking in the footsteps of the clan Ancestors.

     thinking

                    trembling

    electric light

As they walk, repeating the Ancestor's verses, they sing the land into view, recreating the creation. Earlier, the boy had written about his dying—a premature eulogy. He finally went and did it. And the boy wasn't ready. He dropped one word at a time, but he didn't expect the father to follow. And after the tree, the orchard rose in the brilliant air.

I imagine the father who is both "my father" and "not my father" talking to the Aborigines. There was a time before he died, after the cancer had metastasized to his brain, when the whole family gathered around the body of the dying father. And the dying father who had not spoken in months began to speak in a holy gibberish. They did not know he was speaking Dreamtime. They did not know he sang his cancer throughout the room. They did not know he was singing their bodies into existence.

twigs & physics

burn

marks

66

TEARS & THREAD

a chiasmatic singing

The sister and the boy were sitting next to the father's hospital bed. He was supposed to die at any time. It was late at night. The sister nudged the boy. "I think he has died," she said. "No. I think he is sleeping," said the boy and went to the nurse and tried to explain his sister's confusion. "My sister thinks our father has died, but I know he is climbing the tree of his sleeping."

The father reaches into the scrappy branches, a ladder with a rotten rung leaning. His body, tipsy, seared. And there is nothing the boy can do to stop him, not his mandarin prose, not the wonderful distractions, the tangents. He clips the fruit stem as close to the fruit as possible; he twists it, his hand molded around its world. The rip of skin. He breathes the non-air. Stone seeds. The white trails and the nearly translucent flesh. Fear and the satisfying juices.

placenta

of music

glass conception

disturbances

67

Vocal

chords

Bridges

Tariffs
on

air

pencil
markings

on the brain

an avalanche
of deletions

ticking
mechanisms

appliances
made from
musical notes

Year after year the father died. Now he goes back into the earth.
Because the boy cannot live the father's life, he must have his death.
He keeps writing until he has enough words. The ashtray crisscrossed
with songlines. He keeps writing until he has enough words to bury
the father.

III

Epilogue

From the 2009 *Bitter Oleander* Interview

§§§§§§§§§§§§§§§§§§§§§§§§§§§§§§§§

PBR: *In what direction do you or would you like to see your writing take over the next few or so years?*

PL: I will be in the process of composing the Kindle Book. I am not referring to the embedded system for reading electronic books. What I am referring to is the perpetual book we are all in the process of writing—the collective book without boundaries and binding—adaptively vital, exquisitely, pulsingly alive—ever-evolving and generative. The book that kindles the next book, and the next book, and the next. Until it is all a beautiful blaze.

Here is what I suspect: I will be writing a poem and it will turn into a novel. I will be writing a novel and it will turn into a screenplay. I will be writing a screenplay and it will turn into an essay. I will be writing an essay and it will turn into a poem.

I hope my writing will be full of hyphens and contractions—hyphens because of the hybrid nature of what needs to be done and contractions because of the necessity of birth and rebirth.

In most of my last classes, I leave my students with the words of Anaïs Nin, "And the day came when the risk to remain tight in a bud was more painful than the risk it took to blossom." I know my students provide me with the main reason I write: blossoming.

Though it saddens me to arrive at the end of this interview, I know it is over when I have a dream where I am trapped inside a cellar and there is a small hole in the roof through which my daughter lowers rolled-up poems and drops almonds for me to eat. This is how I know I have reached an ending, and this is how I celebrate how it blossoms into multiple beginnings.

At One of My Father's Funerals,
I Was Humphrey Bogart

At one of my father's funerals, I was Humphrey Bogart.
I stood in a trench coat pulling the smoke out of a cigarette. At
one of my father's funerals, he was very talkative—almost inap-
propriately so. "It is amazing," he said. "You just wouldn't believe
it."

At one of my father's funerals, my mother danced. Awk-
ward at first, nearly toppling, then eventually as graceful as fog.
At first her foot seemed to test the solidness of the floor, and
then the tentative attempts. Finally, to the dismay of my aunts,
she twirled dreamily, like an Arthur Murray dance instructor in a
trance.
At one of my father's funerals, we all fell asleep. An elderly
lady gently snored to the rhythm of barely audible church hymns.
At one of my father's funerals, the servants brought in deli-
cious bowls of fruit, and we wept like gods.

At one of my father's funerals, all we could do was talk
about Shelley's heart.

At one of my father's funerals, a woman appeared with
scratches on her hands from having tried to catch too many birds.
At one of my father's funerals, a child bored breathing holes
into the casket. At one of my father's funerals, the river cracked
through the walls—fish leapt into the coffin.

At one of my father's funerals, he poked his head through
a portal. "Now anything is possible," he said.

At one of my father's funerals, Jesus showed up—tortured

and celestial. The synchronized weepers' choreographed tears fell like musical notes.

At one of my father's funerals, he said, "What do I hear for this lovely casket. Barely used."

A man in a grayish robe raised his hand. "Jesus," I said.

At one of my father's funerals, I was older than my father. "You look like hell," he said.

At one of my father's funerals, we thought my uncle brought flowers, but it was really a rash. One of my aunt's came with an alibi.

My father said, "If I am not conscious of my death, then how can I be dead?"

The doctor listed the symptoms and pushed his finger into my father's chest in order to find the heart.

At one of my father's funerals, the bounty hunter wept into his warrant. A fisherman laid a whimsical fish on the coffin.

At one of my father's funerals, a fire started. The tow truck driver arrived with the flowers. At one of my father's funerals, the funeral director dipped a cigarette into embalming fluid. The driver of the hearse was picked up for DWI. The bootlegger comforted me. "They'll never be anyone like your father," he said.

At one of my father's funerals, the tour bus came in with the Alzheimer's patients who were trying to say the right words to the family. The stroke patients tilted beautifully in their card table chairs.

At one of my father's funerals, I developed the power to exchange organs with my dying relatives. When I left the room I had the liver of a drunken uncle. At one of my father's funerals, we read the Romantics and Keats showed up. At one of my father's funerals, I cried, and no one asked me why.

At one of my father's funerals, a man carried an umbrella. A woman carried a packed suitcase. My father announced that he was afraid of falling.

I watched a tear roll down the umbrella.

At one of my father's funerals, we played cards while my father sat in his mahogany drawer. While he was trying to untie the knot in his head, my mother deposited her voice in the cochlea of his ear. The priest said, "Now what are we going to do?"

A girl announced she had had a dream about a traveling funeral.

I pondered a handful of birds.

At one of my father's funerals, Katherine Hepburn showed up. Her beauty seared our brains. A big bold hat tipped over her eye. She had orchid shimmer on her lips.

At one of my father's funerals, a woman showed me her hands and said, "This is what happens when you try to catch birds." I was an adolescent. I announced to the girl, "I keep a book called *Magic* under my bed."

At one of my father's funerals, someone mentioned the frozen dream where all the dream characters are trapped behind a thin layer of ice. Eventually we rowed the coffin across the lake. At one of my father's funerals, my mother inconsolably danced.

My Father's Bio

For a long time, he did not know he was a poet.

He was a farmer and a soldier and a salesman. He sold aluminum siding and vacuum cleaners and Watkins products and diet candy. He was a prison guard and an alcoholic. Almost none of it is a big deal.

My father wanted me to write a book about him. He almost begged. Somehow I couldn't.

Years before, after he read my poetry, he asked if I was on drugs. That's when I became suspicious of critics.

The last five years of my father's life he wrote stories, and he fancied himself a writer. A father walking in the footsteps of the son. Frankly, I had been a little embarrassed by the things he read me, and yet they were read with such enthusiasm I hated to disappoint by my disapproval. I bought him a thesaurus and a dictionary.

After he died he left me with a box of words I haven't been able to read until now.

And now I see all the words I've ever written had always been waiting for me inside the box.

WW II collage excerpt with friends and acquaintances of the author's father.

Patrick Lawler's Bio

I lived in a small place inside the earth. And it was beautiful at times and scary at other times.

I have been a house painter and a floorman in a wiremill; I sold and set up trailers, and I mowed cemeteries (I liked that job because it seemed to get me in touch with destinations). I worked as an orderly in a hospital ("Oh, my gawd," I said), and I worked in a factory ("Oh, my gawd," I said). I prepared income taxes (I liked that job because it gave me a sense of eco-nomy), and I worked in a place that replaced and repaired glass (I liked that job because it gave me a sense of epistemology).

Eventually I was in a classroom with students. I was paid as their teacher, but that surprised me and seemed presumptuous on so many levels.

I hope someday someone will give me a thesaurus and a diction-ary. I don't know if that will be meant as a critique or an acknowl-edgement of possibility.

This is the book that was waiting inside the box. At one level I never wanted it to be published (until Tim gave me the courage, Paul gave me the opportunity, and Jeffrey insisted upon seeing this through to the end). And at another level, it was all I ever really had to say.

Author Bio:

Patrick Lawler has three earlier collections of poetry published: *A Drowning Man is Never Tall Enough* (University of Georgia Press, 1990), *reading a burning book* (Basfal Books, 1994), and *Feeding the Fear of the Earth,* the winner of the Many Mountains Moving poetry book competition (2006). He is the 2010 recipient of the Ronald Sukenick/ABR Prize for Innovative Fiction, and he has books scheduled to appear from Ravenna Books, Four Way Books, and The Bitter Oleander Press. He has received a National Endowment of the Arts Fellowship, two grants from the New York State Foundation for the Arts, and an award from the Constance Saltonstall Foundation for the Arts. His poetry, fiction, and creative nonfiction have appeared in over a hundred journals. In addition, he is the ecopoetry and drama editor of *Many Mountains Moving: a literary journal of diverse contemporary voices.*